Read All About Sharks

GIANT SHARKS

Lynn Stone

The Rourke Corporation, Inc.
Vero Beach, Florida 32964

PHOTO CREDITS
©Tom Campbell: cover, p.6, 10, 16, 20; ©Marty Snyderman: p.4, 15; ©James D. Watt/INNERSPACE VISIONS: p.7; ©Amos Nachoum/ INNERSPACE VISIONS: p.9, 12; ©Gray Adkison/INNERSPACE VISIONS: p.13; ©Doug Perrine: p.18; ©Bruce Rasner/INNERSPACE VISIONS: p.19; ©Lynn M. Stone: p.22

Library of Congress Cataloging-in-Publication Data

Stone, Lynn M.
     Giant sharks / by Lynn M. Stone
          p. cm. — (Read all about sharks)
     Includes index.
     Summary: Briefly describes several of the species of sharks that are more than ten feet long, including the great white shark, tiger shark, whale shark, and basking shark.
     ISBN 0-86593-443-6 (alk. paper)
     1. Sharks—Juvenile literature.   2. Sharks—Size—Juvenile literature.
[1. Sharks.]
I. Title II. Series: Stone, Lynn M. Read all about sharks
QL638.9.S8463 1996
597'.31—dc20   96–7968
                                                                              CIP
                                                                              AC

TABLE OF CONTENTS

Giant Sharks 5

The Biggest Giants 6

Giant Danger 8

Seafood for Giants 11

Meat for Giants 12

Great White Sharks 14

Whale Sharks 17

Tiger Sharks .18

Basking Sharks 20

Glossary 23

Index 24

GIANT SHARKS

Imagine a fish with its jaws on the rim of a basketball hoop and its tail dragging the floor. That fish would have to be 10 feet long—a giant fish!

As many as 40 **species** (SPEE sheez), or kinds, of sharks could be called giants. They reach 10 feet in length.

Among those 40 kinds of giant sharks are six that top 20 feet! These are the true giants.

Giant sharks are much longer and heavier than the people who visit their undersea world.

THE BIGGEST GIANTS

The biggest of the giant sharks are the whale, basking, great white, tiger, Greenland, and great hammerhead. Also in the top ten are the thresher, bigeye thresher, megamouth, and longfin mako.

The 40-foot-long whale shark is the biggest fish in the sea.

The great white shark is the third largest of the sharks.

One giant shark, the megalodon, was probably bigger than any of today's sharks. Scientists know megalodon only from its huge, seven-inch teeth.

Megalodon was perhaps 45 feet long. It may have weighed as much as 10 full-size cars. Megalodon disappeared from the seas thousands of years ago.

GIANT DANGER

Some of the giant sharks can be dangerous to people.

The sharks often considered most dangerous are the great white, tiger, and bull sharks.

Size itself, however, does not make a shark dangerous. The two largest sharks, the whale and basking sharks, are not usually dangerous to people. On the other hand, certain small sharks can pack a mighty bite.

With its fearsome jaws, the great white is considered the most dangerous shark.

SEAFOOD FOR GIANTS

Whale and basking sharks aren't generally dangerous to people because they don't eat large **prey** (PRAY). These sharks feed on **plankton** (PLANK ton). Ocean plankton is a saltwater stew of tiny, floating plants and animals. Whale and basking sharks cruise the sea and swallow huge numbers of plankton every day.

People, of course, are far too big to be plankton, even if they are floating in the sea. Whatever divers look like to these giant sharks, they do not look like food.

Holding his breath, a diver poses with a huge, but generally harmless, whale shark.

MEAT FOR GIANTS

Most giant sharks are meat eaters. Depending upon the kind of shark, they eat fish, squid, sea turtles, or even seals.

In a sailor's tale from the 1700's, a shark swallowed a man whole. Soon afterward, the shark threw the man up, leaving him unharmed.

A great white shark lunges from the sea for a piece of meat.

With a diver below, a great hammerhead gobbles up a jackfish.

Could a huge shark actually swallow a man whole? Yes, but it's not likely. In fact, even shark bites are rare.

GREAT WHITE SHARKS

Great white sharks are the largest of the truly dangerous sharks. The longest great white known was nearly 30 feet long. It may have weighed 10,000 pounds.

Great whites often catch seals and **sea lions** (SEE li unz). Sometimes they swallow their prey whole.

Great white sharks are found in nearly all oceans. They are common off the shore of Northern California. They find seals plentiful there.

Great white sharks often prey on seals and sea lions, which they sometimes swallow whole.

WHALE SHARKS

The whale shark was well named. At 40 feet in length, it's about the size of a sperm or humpback whale.

The whale shark has a broad saucerlike mouth. That huge mouth can be eight feet across. Like a giant vacuum cleaner, it sifts the plankton from thousands of gallons of seawater each day.

Whale sharks cruise the surface of warm oceans. Sometimes they collide with ships.

A giant whale shark, trailed by a diver, cruises near the ocean surface.

TIGER SHARKS

The tiger shark was named for its tigerlike stripes. The stripes fade away as the sharks grow and age. The biggest of the known tiger sharks, more than 20 feet in length, are almost stripeless.

A tiger shark swims slowly over the shallow, sandy ocean bottom in the Bahama Islands.

A diver photographs the extremely rare megamouth shark. The megamouth has been seen only twice!

Tigers are the fourth largest kind of shark. They are the second largest of the so-called man-eating sharks. One 18-foot tiger shark, caught off South Carolina, weighed 3,360 pounds.

Tiger sharks like warmer seas than the great white.

BASKING SHARKS

The basking shark is named for its habit of resting—or **basking** (BAS king)—near the ocean surface. Sometimes this shark basks upside down at the surface.

The basking shark is the second largest known species of shark. The biggest basking shark on record was just under 40 feet in length. That shark probably weighed about 8,000 pounds.

Basking sharks that were seen swimming together may have started sea monster legends among sailors.

A basking shark's huge mouth filters plankton from several tons of seawater each day.

GLOSSARY

basking (BAS king) — resting in a warm, pleasant place

plankton (PLANK ton) — tiny, floating plants and animals in the sea and other bodies of water

prey (PRAY) — an animal that is hunted by other animals for food

sea lions (SEE li unz) — a group of sea mammals that are cousins of seals

species (SPEE sheez) — within a group of closely related animals, one certain kind, such as a *basking* shark.

This sea lion is safe now, but in the sea below may lurk a great white shark.

INDEX

divers   11

people   11

plankton   11, 17

prey   11, 14

scientists   6

sea lions   14

seals   14

shark bites   13

sharks

   basking   8, 11, 20

   bigeye thresher   6

   bull   8

great hammerhead   6

great white   6, 8, 14

Greenland   6

longfin mako   6

megalodon   6, 7

megamouth   6

thresher   6

tiger   6, 8, 18

whale   6, 8, 11, 17

teeth   7